STEM *trailblazer* BIOS

MINECRAFT CREATOR

MARKUS "NOTCH" PERSSON

KARI CORNELL

Lerner Publications
Minneapolis

To Theo, the most dedicated and creative video game enthusiast I know.

Lerner Publications Company
A division of Lerner Publishing Group, Inc.
241 First Avenue North
Minneapolis, MN 55401 USA

For reading levels and more information, look up this title at www.lernerbooks.com.

Content consultant: Dave Culyba, assistant teaching professor at Carnegie Mellon's Entertainment Technology Center

Library of Congress Cataloging-in-Publication Data

Cornell, Kari, author.
    Minecraft creator Markus "Notch" Persson / Kari Cornell.
      pages cm. — (STEM trailblazer bios)
    Audience: Ages 7–11.
    Audience: Grades 4 to 6.
    Includes bibliographical references and index.
    ISBN 978-1-4677-9526-5 (lb : alk. paper) — ISBN 978-1-4677-9713-9 (pb : alk. paper) — ISBN 978-1-4677-9714-6 (eb pdf)
    1. Persson, Markus, 1979—Juvenile literature. 2. Computer programmers—Sweden—Biography—Juvenile literature. 3. Minecraft (Game)—Juvenile literature. 4. Computer games—Design—Juvenile literature. I. Title. II. Series: STEM trailblazer bios.
    HD8039.D372S94 2016
    794.8092—dc23
                                                            2015023001

Manufactured in the United States of America
1 – BP – 12/31/15

Main body text set in Adrianna Regular 13/22. Typeface provided by Chank.

CONTENTS

Persson's childhood hobbies like playing with LEGO bricks influenced his career as an adult.

A BOY AND HIS COMPUTER

Markus Persson has been having the same dream since he was a boy. In the dream, he is playing with friends in the woods near his childhood home. Markus loses his way and begins to realize he is truly lost. Finally, he stumbles upon a path that leads him home.

Parts of this dream have made their way into *Minecraft*, the unique and popular video game Markus designed in 2009. The game includes LEGO-like blocks that players use to build whatever they like. It has sold better than anyone—even Persson—ever expected.

EARLY YEARS

Markus Alexej Persson was born in Stockholm, Sweden, on June 1, 1979. His mother was a nurse. His father worked for the Swedish railroad and loved tinkering with computers. Markus grew up in Edsbyn, a small town in the Swedish countryside.

Markus's hometown of Edsbyn, Sweden, had plenty of land and woods for him to explore.

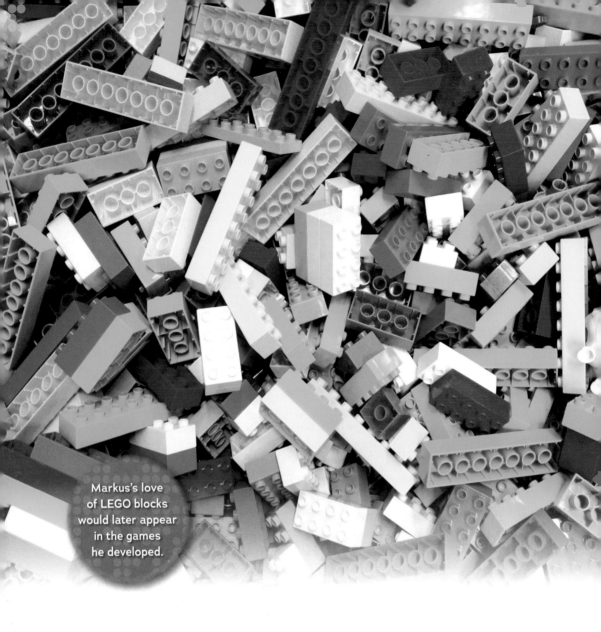

Markus's love of LEGO blocks would later appear in the games he developed.

He and his friends spent their summers playing in the woods. In winter, Markus spent hours playing with LEGO blocks. He built complex spaceships and cars, only to tear them apart to create something new.

When Markus was seven, his father bought a Commodore 128, one of the best personal computers available at the time. Markus and his father spent the whole evening reading through the manual and plugging in cables. The computer came with a few games, but Markus was much more interested in the simple **programming** instructions included in the manual. When he typed in a **code**, he could make the computer do things like scroll text up or down on the screen. He also began typing code that was printed on the backs of video game magazines.

An ad for the Commodore 128, a popular computer in the 1980s that Markus used to learn how to program

to match the versatility, expandability and higher intelligence of the new Commodore 128
(and it costs less too).

TECH TALK

"My sister would read the lines out to me and I would tap them into the computer. After a while, I figured out that if you didn't type out exactly what they told you then something different would happen when you finally ran the game. That sense of power was intoxicating."

—*Markus Persson*

Within a year, Markus was writing his own **computer programs** for simple text adventure games. In this type of game, players read along on the screen and type specific text to move through the story. At first, Markus didn't know how to save what he had done, so each time he turned off the computer, his program was lost. But Markus didn't care. He would just power it up and start all over again. He loved learning how to control the computer.

BIRTH OF A GAMER

In 1986, Markus and his family moved to Stockholm. Markus had a hard time fitting in at his new school. Eventually he made a few friends who were as interested in computers as he was. Together they played video games, including *The Bard's Tale*. They also played role-playing board games, creating their own fantasy worlds, complete with monsters, dragons, and elves. Markus loved these games and often led the group by inventing the stories and making challenges for the other players.

Role-playing games allowed Markus to be creative and connect with friends.

Programming and playing computer games helped Markus cope during troubled times at home.

When Markus was twelve, his parents divorced and his father moved away. Markus took his mind off these troubles by playing video games and programming. Sometimes Markus was so focused on programming that he didn't want to go to school. He would tell his mother that he didn't feel well and then spend the entire day in front of the computer.

Although Markus did very well in school, few classes interested him. At fourteen, Markus already knew that he wanted a job creating video games. The one computer programming class at his high school was too easy. On the first day of class, Markus sat down and programmed his own version of the computer game *Pong*, based on Ping-Pong. His teacher saw his work and told him he didn't have to come back until the last day for the final test. Markus easily earned an A in the class.

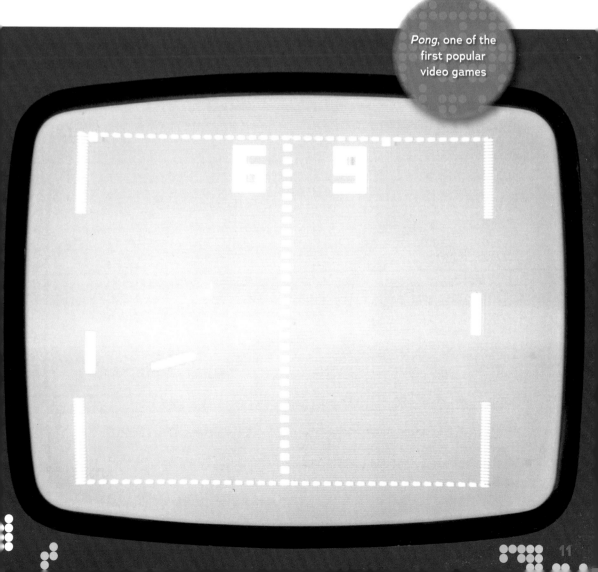

Pong, one of the first popular video games

Chapter 2

Persson almost always wears his signature fedora when he's in public.

BECOMING A
PROGRAMMER

Persson left high school in 1997 to take a job as a computer programmer, but not at a game company. He grew bored with the job and left after about six months.

Soon after, a **recession** hit and jobs in the computer industry became much harder to find.

He lived with his mother, created his own games, and entered computer-game programming competitions. He wasn't making any money, but he was getting better at writing code. His mother encouraged him to take programming classes to get him out of the house. He took a class in a programming language called C++.

Persson worked for a couple of years at a game **distributor** called Gamefederation. Then, in 2004, he landed his dream job. He was hired as a programmer at the popular video game company Midasplayer, later called King.com. Persson was one of the first programmers they hired.

TECH TALK

"What separated Markus from other deve King was he had a deep knowledge about Markus had a little bit of everything in him like a one-man show."

—*Tom Cheshire, writer for* Wired

He couldn't believe he was finally working as a video game programmer. His first challenge was to learn the programming language ActionScript. He picked it up quickly and impressed his coworkers with his skills.

BENDING THE RULES

Before long, Persson was teaching new employees how to write code for games. One of these employees was Jacob Porser, and the two quickly became friends. Porser and Persson shared a passion for video games. They also both loved playing the card game Magic: The Gathering. Porser's dream was to develop a video game based on Magic. He and Persson spent lunch hours and time after work talking about how they might develop it.

A player holds Magic: The Gathering cards.

Meanwhile, Persson was busy working on his own new games in his free time. But Midasplayer had rules against employees developing their own games. After posting his latest game on the company network and inviting coworkers to try it, Persson was fired.

Persson wasn't too upset about having to leave Midasplayer, however. He had learned a lot in the four years he worked there, and he had developed more than twenty-five games. But he was ready to move on. More than anything, Persson wanted to be in charge of his own games. He wanted to have the freedom to create interesting games he liked instead of worrying about how games would sell.

Persson quickly found a new job at jAlbum, an online personal photo album site. He became friends with a business **executive** at the company, Carl Manneh. Because the company was not in the business of creating video games, Persson was free to develop his games on his own time. And that's just what he did.

Carl Manneh, who worked with Persson at jAlbum

Chapter 3

Young players participate in a *Minecraft* tournament on August 9, 2014.

MINECRAFT
MANIA

On a quiet weekend in May 2009, Persson sat down at his home computer and wrote the code for a game he had been thinking about for a while. When he was done, the game didn't quite look finished, but he liked it that way. In fact, he left parts of the game unfinished so players could have a role in how the game developed.

Persson's new game, called *Minecraft*, provided a digital world where players are free to explore the landscape. Most players decide to settle down and begin building with a supply of bricks that they can use to create whatever they like. They "mine" for resources like gold, wool, or wood. The only real object of the game is to finish building a secure shelter before nightfall, when monsters and zombies come to attack. Players are also free to work in creative mode, where monsters don't exist.

Minecraft's simple world and the freedom for players to explore made it an instant hit.

TECH TALK

"Infinite power just isn't very interesting. . . . It's much more fun when you have a limited tool set to use against the odds. Usually, a new player to *Minecraft* doesn't make it through the first night. They're just not prepared for the danger. It's a harsh lesson but it establishes the rules."

—*Markus Persson*

AN INSTANT SUCCESS

On May 17, 2009, Persson released *Minecraft* online through TIGSource, a site for game players and creators. Almost immediately he was selling about four hundred **downloads** of the game per day at a price of six dollars each. In the first year, *Minecraft* sold about twenty thousand downloads. By the end of 2010, Persson was selling that many downloads each day. He was amazed by the game's instant success.

The game was selling like crazy, and it wasn't even finished. On TIGSource, players gave ideas and feedback about the game. Every Friday, Persson read the player comments as he updated the game with new features. By inviting players to have a say in the shaping of *Minecraft*, Persson earned the respect and loyalty of millions of fans.

As *Minecraft* grew in popularity, fans began to gather each year for a convention called MineCon.

TECH TALK

"There are game-design rules that are carved in stone—about teaching people to play, having objectives, a character, an adversary. *Minecraft* threw all that away. . . . There is an active, rabid community of gamers who create "mods": everything from playable musical instruments to falling meteors to tornadoes."

—*Peter Molyneux, game designer*

In 2010, Persson decided to adopt the name Notch when he was online. Notch was the name he always used in TIGSource, and he decided to use it whenever he communicated with fans and players. Using a different name made the usually shy Persson more comfortable voicing his opinions on video games. Today most fans know Persson as Notch.

The popularity of *Minecraft* made Persson a household name among gamers.

Chapter 4

Programmers at work in the Mojang company office

A NEW ERA

For years, Persson and Porser had dreamed of starting their own game development company. In late 2010, they finally quit their day jobs to start Mojang, which means "gadget" in Swedish. They hired Carl Manneh, Persson's friend from jAlbum, to handle the business details, while Persson and Porser focused on game development. Mojang was soon making a profit, as sales for *Minecraft* continued to climb. Within the company's first year, they hired several new employees. *Minecraft* was Mojang's focus, but Persson also encouraged Porser to develop his idea for a computer game based on Magic: The Gathering.

As *Minecraft's* popularity grew, the game won several industry awards and praise from game developers.

Minecraft had become a worldwide phenomenon. Fans gathered online to talk about the game. They shared instructions for the easiest ways to make different items in *Minecraft*. Players also posted photos of their own *Minecraft* creations, including the Taj Mahal, the Eiffel Tower, and even planet Earth.

Passionate fans sent Persson hundreds of comments each day about ways to improve *Minecraft*. After a while, this became too much for him. In 2011, he handed control of *Minecraft* development and updates to Jens Bergensten, the lead **game developer** at Mojang.

Persson at work with other game developers at Mojang.

REAL-LIFE PROBLEMS

In 2011, *Minecraft* sales were continuing to climb, and Persson had recently gotten married. Then, a few days before Christmas, Persson learned that his father had taken his own life. Persson was devastated. In the months following his father's death, Persson and his wife divorced.

He focused on new projects to keep his mind off his problems. He began work on a new game called *0x10c* The new game was based on *Minecraft* but set in space. The game included many advanced features, such as a computer that players could program themselves. Eventually, Persson gave up on *0x10c*. He decided he wasn't ready to tackle such a large project.

Meanwhile, *Minecraft*'s popularity continued to grow. In November 2013, Mojang hosted more than seventy-five hundred fans, many dressed as their favorite *Minecraft* characters, at a convention in Orlando, Florida. By June 2014, *Minecraft* had sold a whopping fifty-four million copies. Mojang partnered with LEGO and other toy companies. *Minecraft* LEGO kits, books, foam swords, and costumes filled store shelves.

Fans pose with *Minecraft*-style swords at the 2013 *Minecraft* convention.

Persson addresses the audience during opening ceremonies at the 2013 *Minecraft* convention.

But all the hype was starting to wear Persson down. He was tired of hearing fan complaints about the game. He also learned that some fans were illegally making money off *Minecraft*. In September 2014, Persson sold Mojang to Microsoft for $2.5 billion. Fans and Mojang employees were shocked by the news, but Persson made no apologies. He thanked his fans for their support through the years. He told them that they would always be the true owners of *Minecraft*.

Persson tries to focus on having fun to make up for all the time he spent working when he was younger.

SOMETHING NEW

Persson and Porser have started a new game development company called Rubberbrain, based in Stockholm. Persson tries to focus on having fun instead of trying to create a game that is better than *Minecraft*. Even Persson believes it's not possible for him to develop a game that comes close. Fans will just have to wait and see.

TIMELINE

1979

Markus Alexej Persson is born in Stockholm, Sweden. Soon after, the family moves to Edsbyn, a small town in the countryside.

1986

Persson's father brings home a Commodore 128 computer. The family moves back to Stockholm.

1987

Persson programs his first text adventure game.

1997

Persson leaves high school to get a job as a programmer.

1999

Persson quits his job just as technology companies stop hiring.

2009

Persson develops *Minecraft* and releases it on TIGSource.

2010

Persson and Jacob Porser start their own company called Mojang.

2011

Persson hands control of *Minecraft* to Jens Bergensten, Mojang's lead developer.

2014

Minecraft sales hit fifty-four million copies. Microsoft buys *Minecraft*.

2015

Persson and Porser start a new gaming company called Rubberbrain.

SOURCE NOTES

8 Simon Parkin, "The Creator," *New Yorker*, April 5, 2013, http://www.newyorker.com/tech/elements/the-creator.

13 Tom Cheshire, "Changing the Game: How Notch Made Minecraft a Cult Hit," *Wired*, September 15, 2014, http://www.wired.co.uk/magazine/archive/2012/07/features/changing-the-game.

18 Simon Parkin, "The Creator."

20 David Peisner, "The Wizard of Minecraft," *Rolling Stone*, May 7, 2014, http://www.rollingstone.com/culture/news/the-wizard-of-minecraft-20140507.

25 Cheshire, "Changing the Game."

GLOSSARY

code
a series of letters, numbers, and symbols that a computer can understand

computer programs
sets of step-by-step instructions that tell a computer to do something

distributor
a company that sends products to stores or websites to be sold

downloads
copies moved from one location, such as a website, to another, such as a personal computer

executive
a person in a business who makes decisions about how the business operates

game developer
a company or person who creates video games

programming
using code to tell a computer to do something

recession
a time when businesses are not hiring and many people lose their jobs

FURTHER INFORMATION

BOOKS

Kaplan, Arie. *The Crazy Careers of Video Game Designers*. Minneapolis: Lerner Publications, 2014. From design to animation, discover what it takes to create video games.

Milton, Stephanie, Paul Soares Jr. and Jordan Maron. *Minecraft Essential Handbook*. New York: Scholastic, 2013. Enter the world of *Minecraft* with this beginner's handbook.

Orr, Tamra. *Markus "Notch" Persson, Creator of Minecraft*. Kennett Square, PA: Purple Toad, 2015. Read more about Markus Persson's life and work as a video game developer.

WEBSITES

Code Monster
http://www.crunchzilla.com/code-monster
Try your hand at coding with the help of Code Monster.

Minecraft
https://minecraft.net
Visit the official *Minecraft* website for a description of the game and a running tally of the number of copies sold.

Minecraft Wiki
http://minecraft.gamepedia.com/Tutorials
Build your *Minecraft* skills with these tutorials for surviving the first day, building shelters, exploring, and more.

LERNER

SOURCE

Expand learning beyond the printed book. Download free, complementary educational resources for this book from our website, www.lerneresource.com.

INDEX

ABOUT THE AUTHOR

Kari Cornell is a freelance writer and editor who lives with her husband, two sons, and dog in Minneapolis, Minnesota. She writes about people who have found a way to do what they love. When she's not writing, she likes tinkering in the garden, cooking, and making something clever out of nothing. Learn more about her work at karicornell.wordpress.com.